A Paw
in my
Heart
Picture Book

Michelle Huirama

This
Book
Belongs
to

_____

_____

For every
little heart
that's ever had
to say
goodbye.

May you always remember
the wagging tails,
soft purrs,
and warm cuddles
that filled your days
with joy.

Even when your
pet isn't near,
their love
stays forever
in your heart.

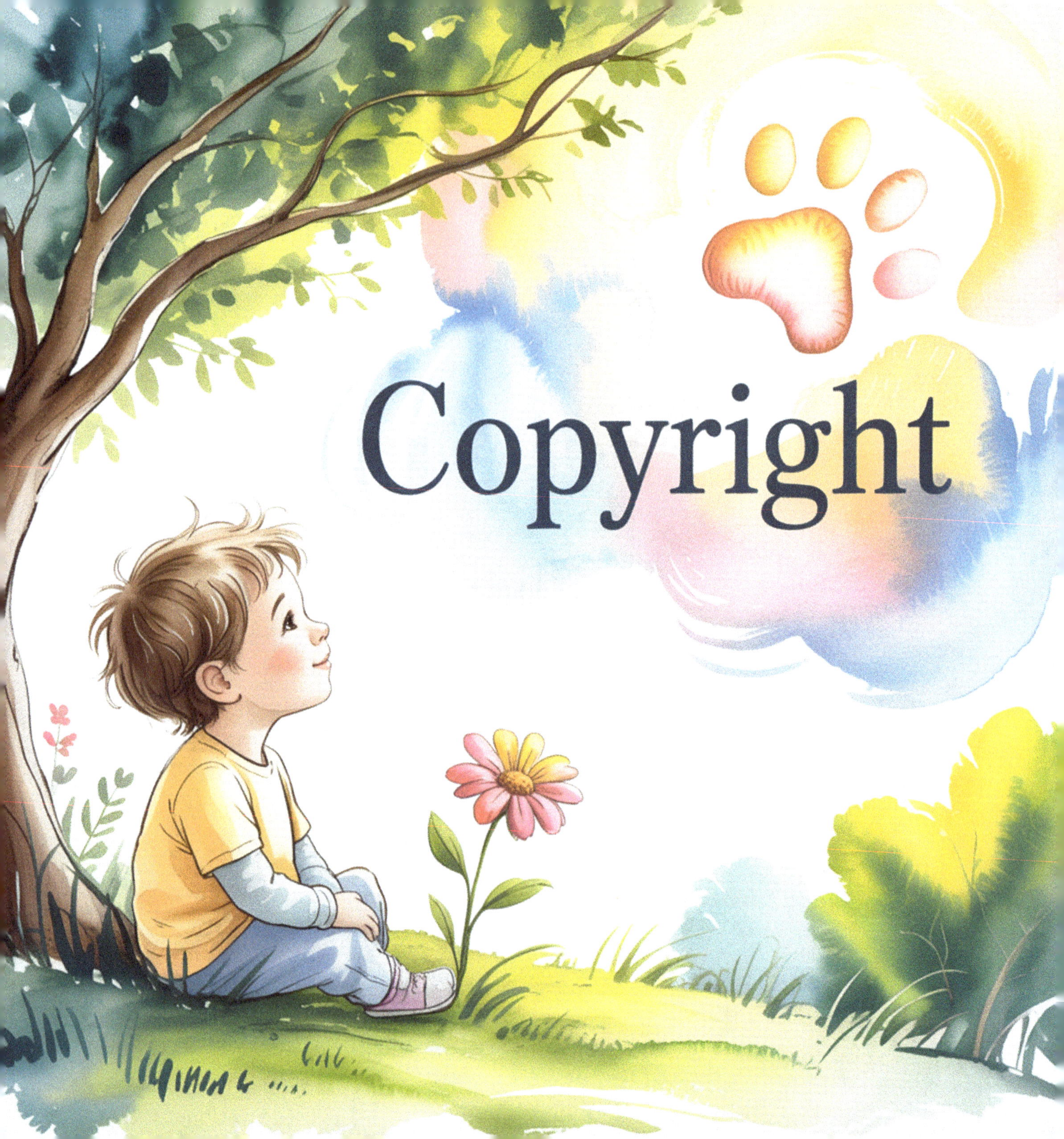
Copyright

Book Cover by Tukotuku Publishing

Illustrations by Tukotuku Publishing

First edition 2025

Print ISBN:978-1-991366-17-7

Ebook ISBN:978-1-991366-18-4

This
is my pet.

My best friend.
My cuddle buddy.
My tail-wagger.
My whisker-kisser.

We played
hide and seek.

And ran in the grass
then snuggled every night.

But one morning
My pet didn't wake up

The house was quiet.
My heart was too.

I felt sad. Then mad.
Then nothing at all.

I didn't want to talk,
I didn't want to play

I told Mom
how much I missed them.

"She said, It's okay
to feel everything."

We talked about the time
they chewed dad's slipper....

...and the time they
barked at the toaster...

I made a box
just for them.

I put in it, a photo, their collar,
and my favorite drawing...

I drew us running,
snuggling, and smiling

I added
hearts and stars.

We planted a flower
where they liked to
nap in the sun..

We lit a candle,
then we told stories.
And said thank you
for being in our lives.

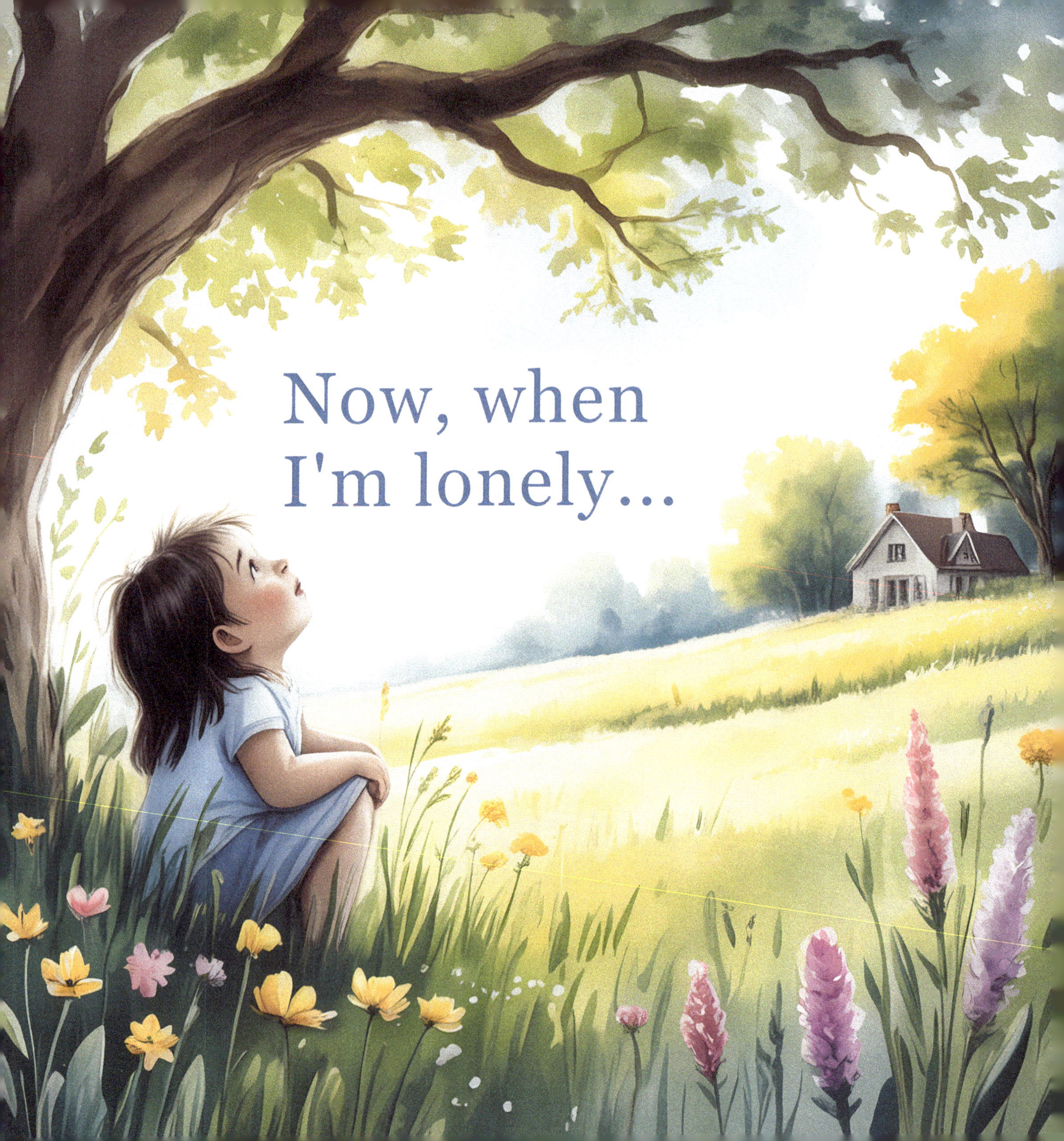
Now, when
I'm lonely...

I remember
the loving paw
in my heart..

Sometimes,
I hear their bark
in the wind.

Or feel their
whiskers
in my dreams..

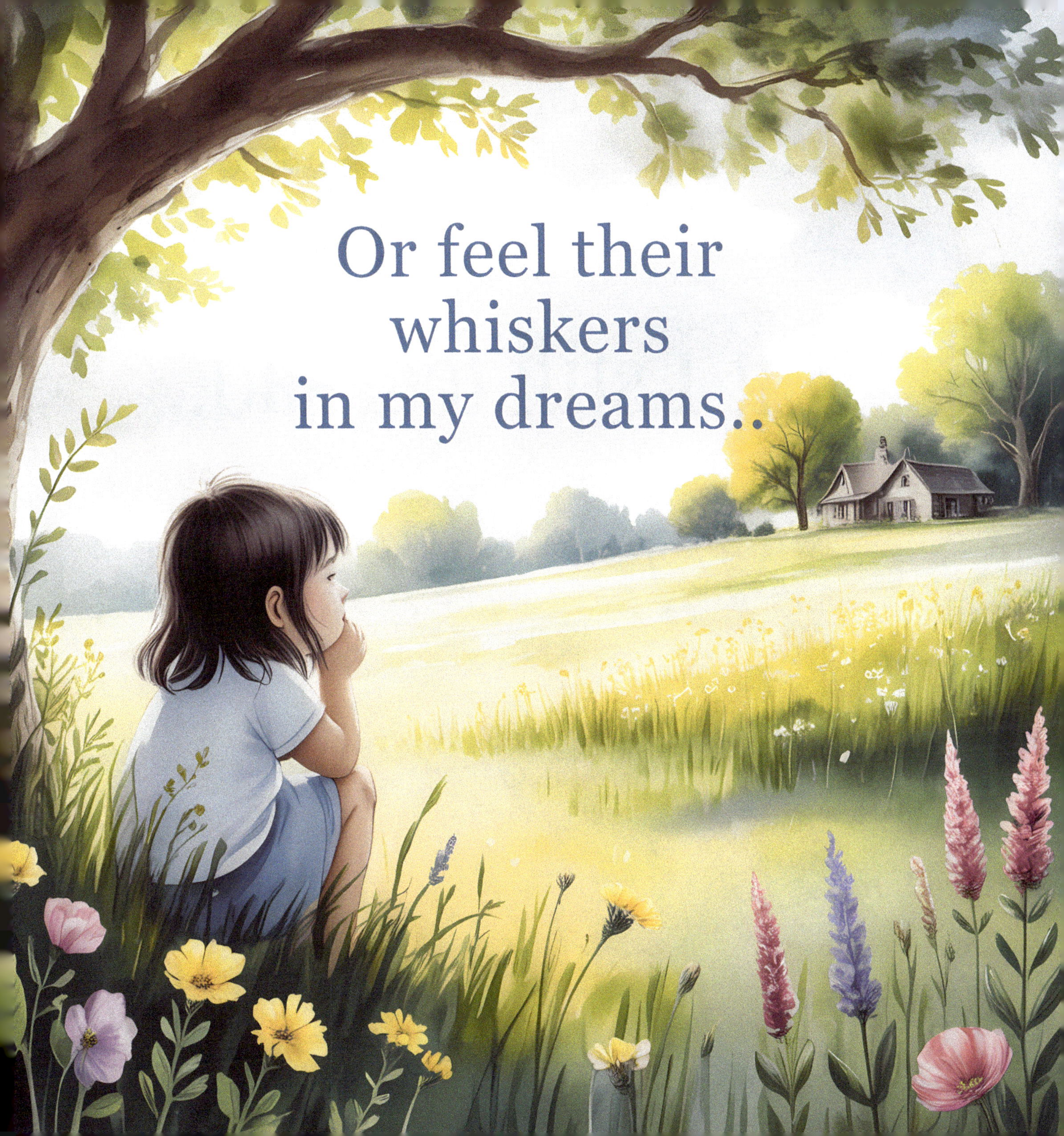

But I still feel sad..

But it's okay to smile too.
Love never really leaves.

I think, One day,
I might have another pet

It's won't be the same.
But it will still be special..

I know that
wherever I go,
that my pet
is with me..

In the giggles.
In the cuddles.
In the quiet.

A paw in my heart.
forever and ever..

This Space
is just for you

A place to Remember

To
Celebrate

and
feel close

To the friend

Who left a paw in your heart

So let's remember them

With
Love

Draw a picture of your pet.

Write a Message

Just for them

Draw your favorite memory.

this is my pet.

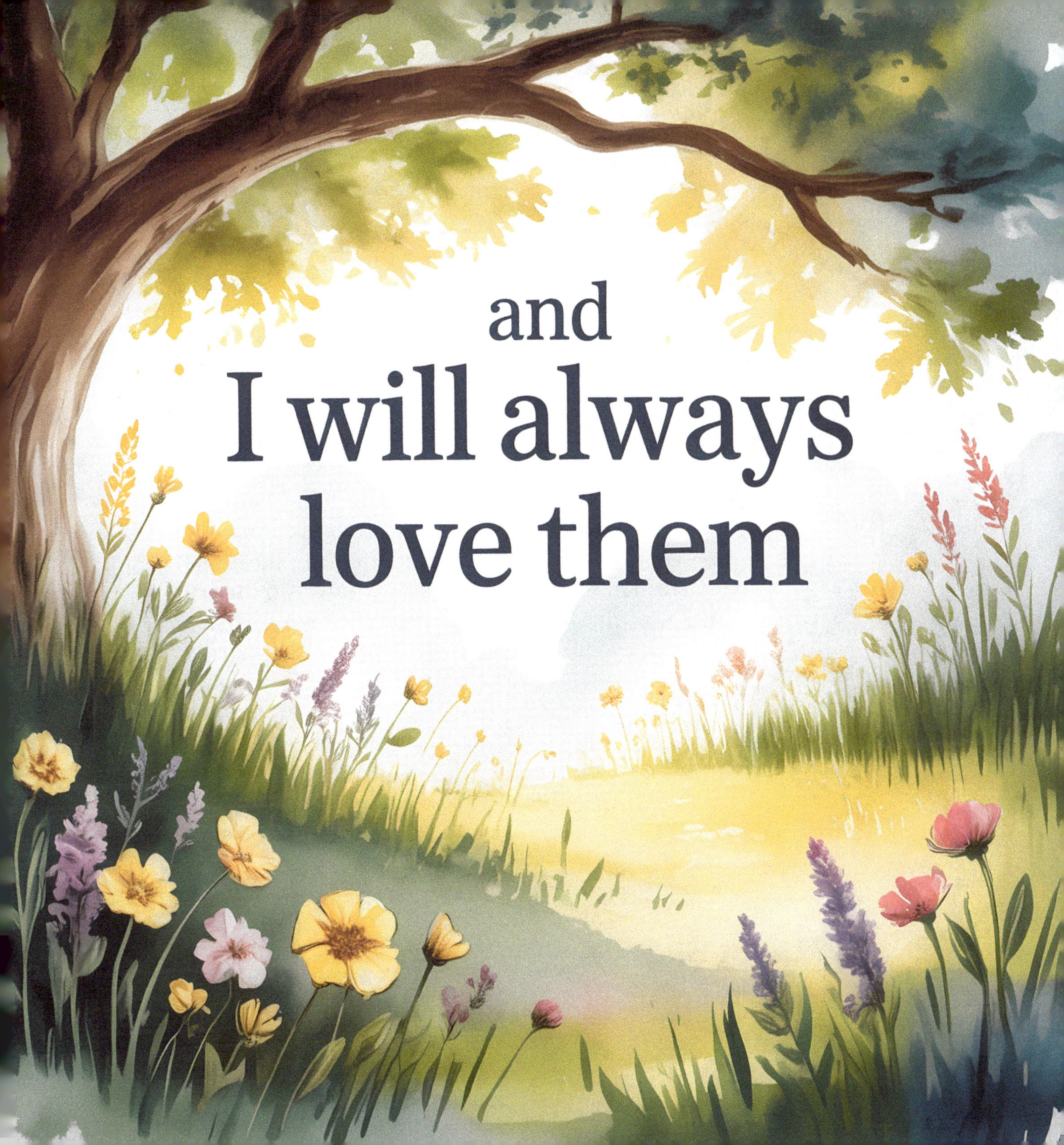

and
I will always
love them

A Note for your Heart

When someone we love — like a special pet leaves us, it can feel like our heart has a missing piece.
But little by little, as we remember the cuddles, the playtimes, and the love we shared...
something amazing happens.
That missing piece becomes a memory, and that memory becomes part of who we are.
Our hearts grow.
And the love we gave — and felt — stays with us, always.
Wherever you go, whatever you do, your pet's paw will walk beside you... tucked safely in your heart.

The
END

Written with empathy and care, this story reminds families that saying goodbye doesn't mean forgetting... It means remembering with love.

A note for grown-ups:

Supporting your child through pet loss

Losing a pet can be a child's first real experience with grief —
and it can feel confusing, overwhelming, or even scary.
This book was designed to help your child explore their emotions
in a safe and creative way.
Here's how you can support them as they grieve:

Validate their Feelings

Children may express sadness, anger, guilt, or even relief. All of these are normal.

Let your child know it's okay to feel what they're feeling — and that grief doesn't have a timeline.

"I miss [pet's name] too.

It's okay to feel sad. I'm here for you."

Talk Honestly About Death

Use age-appropriate language. Avoid confusing phrases like "went to sleep" — instead, gently explain that all living beings have a life cycle. Honest conversations build trust and emotional resilience.

Create space for expression

Create Space for Expression Encourage creative outlets — drawing, journaling, storytelling, or even role-playing. Let them choose how they'd like to honor and remember their pet.

Rituals Can Help

Creating a memory box, planting a flower, or holding a simple ceremony can give children a sense of closure and a tangible way to say goodbye.

Model
healthy grieving

If you're grieving it's okay
to show it.
When children see you
sharing your emotions openly,
it reasures them that
sadness is part of love —
not something to hide..

Most importantly,
Their pet may be gone,
but the bond they shared
will always be part
of who they are.

With love,
Michelle Huirama

Let's Meet

Michelle Huirama

Hi, I'm Michelle — children's author, gentle grief-guide,
and believer in the quiet power of stories.
I write heartfelt stories and picture books that help children navigate
big emotions like love, loss, and letting go. My stories are soft spaces
where young readers (and their grown-ups) can explore feelings,
find comfort, and begin to heal — one page at a time.
My book, A Paw in My Heart, was inspired by the simple truth that
pets are family — and saying goodbye to them is never easy. What
began as one story of loss has blossomed into a whole series of
gentle grief books for children, each one dedicated to honoring love
that stays even after someone we love is gone.
When I'm not writing, you'll find me curled up with my kids and
animals, walking in nature,
or thinking about the next story I want to tell.
Thanks for stopping by. I hope my books bring warmth to your heart,
hope to your home, and a little extra light
to anyone missing someone they love.

Ko Tukotuku te Reikura
Ko Tamainupo te Hapu
Ko Karioi te Maunga
Ko Waikato te Ipukarea
Ko Tainui te Waka

Hearts that Remember

This Book is part of a gentle grief series for little ones who are learning to love, lose, and remember.

Hearts
that
Remember
Series

Has been created for
children up to 6 years of age

When little hearts experience big loss, they need soft spaces to feel, remember, and heal.

Hearts That Remember is a tender picture book series lovingly created to help young children understand grief after losing someone special— like a pet, grandparent, parent, sibling, or friend.

Each book offers comfort through simple words, soft imagery, and age-appropriate storytelling that honors both the sadness and the love that remains. With recurring nature themes, meaningful rituals, and heartwarming illustrations, these books gently guide children through their feelings and remind them that love never really leaves —it lives on in memories, in stories, and in the heart.

More Books
from
Michelle Huirama

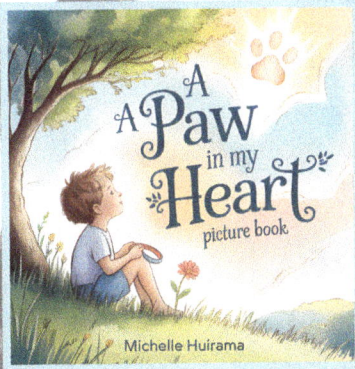

A **Paw** in my **Heart**
picture book
Michelle Huirama

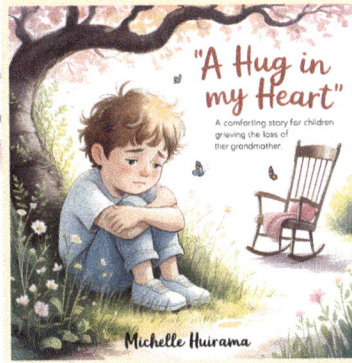

"A Hug in my Heart"
A comforting story for children grieving the loss of their grandmother
Michelle Huirama

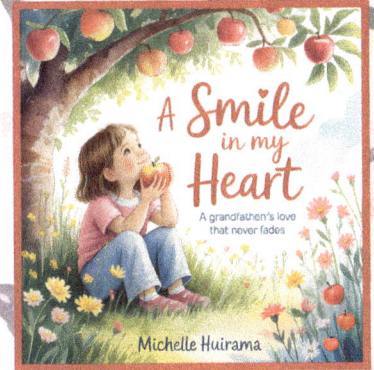

A **Smile** in my **Heart**
A grandfather's love that never fades
Michelle Huirama

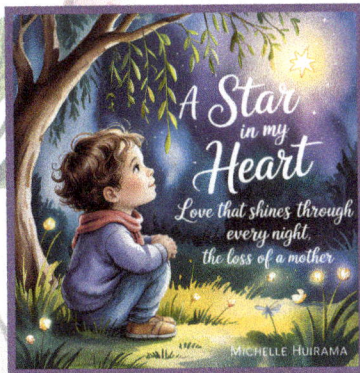

A **Star** in my **Heart**
Love that shines through every night, the loss of a mother
MICHELLE HUIRAMA

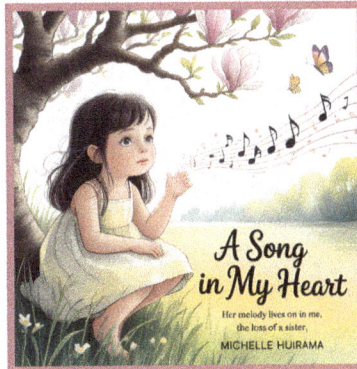

A **Song** in My **Heart**
Her melody lives on in me, the loss of a sister.
MICHELLE HUIRAMA

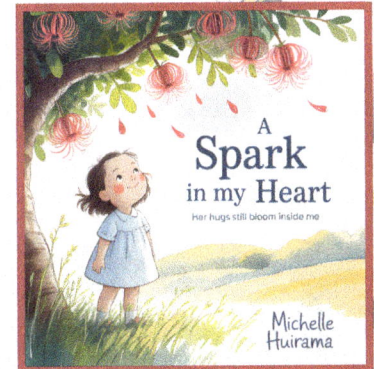

A **Spark** in my **Heart**
Her hugs still bloom inside me
Michelle Huirama

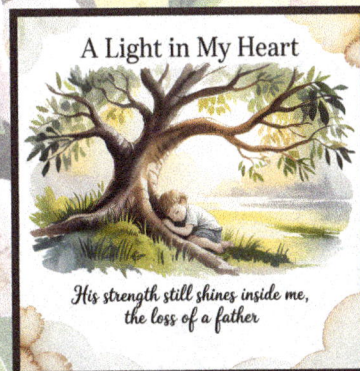

A Light in My Heart
His strength still shines inside me, the loss of a father

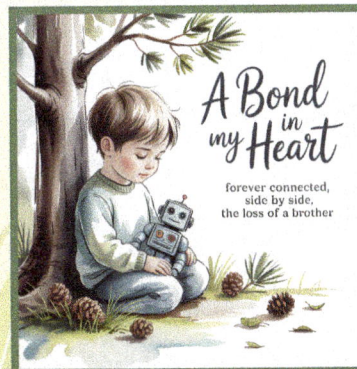

A **Bond** in my **Heart**
forever connected, side by side, the loss of a brother

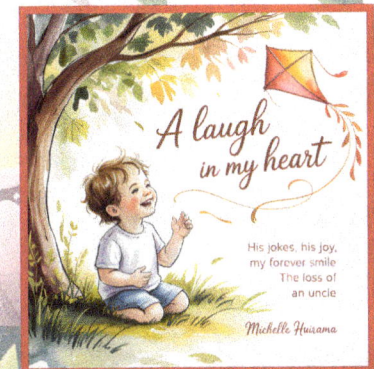

A **laugh** in my heart
His jokes, his joy, my forever smile
The loss of an uncle
Michelle Huirama

"Love That Stays" is a healing grief series for children aged 7 and up. When someone we love is gone, grief becomes the shape love takes. This gentle series helps kids navigate loss—whether it's a grandparent, parent, sibling, friend, or pet—through heartfelt stories, creative activities, and emotional support. With journaling, memory-making, and mindfulness woven into every book, Love That Stays reminds children that grief isn't about forgetting—it's about remembering, growing, and carrying love with them always.